CATS SET V
The Designer Cats

BENGAL CATS

Jill C. Wheeler

ABDO Publishing Company

visit us at
www.abdopublishing.com

Published by ABDO Publishing Company, 8000 West 78th Street, Edina, Minnesota 55439.
Copyright © 2011 by Abdo Consulting Group, Inc. International copyrights reserved in
all countries. No part of this book may be reproduced in any form without written
permission from the publisher. The Checkerboard Library™ is a trademark and logo of
ABDO Publishing Company.

Printed in the United States of America, North Mankato, Minnesota.
092010
012011

 PRINTED ON RECYCLED PAPER

Cover Photo: Photo by Helmi Flick
Interior Photos: Animals Animals p. 7; Photo by Helmi Flick pp. 5, 11, 13, 15, 16, 17, 21;
    iStockphoto p. 20; Peter Arnold pp. 9, 19

Series Coordinator: Heidi M.D. Elston
Editors: Heidi M.D. Elston, Megan M. Gunderson
Cover & Interior Design: Neil Klinepier
Production Layout: Jaime Martens

Library of Congress Cataloging-in-Publication Data

Wheeler, Jill C., 1964-
  Bengal cats / Jill C. Wheeler.
      p. cm. -- (Cats. Set V, Designer cats)
  Includes bibliographical references and index.
  ISBN 978-1-60453-728-4 (alk. paper)
  1. Bengal cat--Juvenile literature. I. Title.
  SF449.B45W44 2010
  636.8'22--dc22
                                    2009021144

Thinking about a Designer Cat?
**Some communities have laws that regulate hybrid animal ownership. Be sure
to check with your local authorities before buying a hybrid kitten.**

CONTENTS

WILD TO MILD

Cats are among the most popular pets in the world. All cats belong to the family **Felidae**. This family includes wildcats and tame cats of all sizes.

There are more than 30 different **breeds** of **domestic** cats. And, there are many mixes of those breeds. Among those mixed breeds are several designer, or **hybrid**, cats. Breeders create designer cats to look like a wildcat but have the personality of a domestic cat.

One of the most popular designer cats is the Bengal cat. It is a cross between a wildcat called the Asian leopard cat and a domestic house cat. The name *Bengal* comes from the Asian leopard cat's scientific name, *Felis bengalensis*.

Bengal cats first became popular because of their appearance. These small domestic cats look like some big wildcats.

ASIAN LEOPARD CATS

Asian leopard cats are native to southern Asia. They are found from southern India east through Thailand and into China. Asian leopard cats often live near water in jungles, **brush**, forests, or **plains**.

These small wildcats weigh up to 15 pounds (7 kg). They have longer legs and bodies than **domestic** cats. To see better at night, they have large eyes. Most Asian leopard cats are tan to orange colored. They have dark spots and a white belly.

Asian leopard cats are excellent swimmers and climbers. They are also skilled **nocturnal** hunters. Their diet includes **rodents** and small birds.

For many years, humans have hunted and trapped these beautiful wildcats. Their coats are highly desirable to those in the fur trade. Still, scientists do not believe Asian leopard cats are in danger of extinction. However, human activity continues to destroy their natural **habitat**. So, their numbers may be threatened in the future.

Asian leopard cat

DOMESTIC CATS

In America, house cats are believed to have arrived with European settlers. The animals were welcomed aboard ships headed for America. They helped control mice and rats during the long voyage.

Once in America, cats continued their role as workers. Over time, people began to think of them as pets.

Today's house cats can be short-haired or long-haired. All are skilled hunters. And, they have been known to learn simple commands.

Several **domestic** cat **breeds** have been ancestors of the Bengal cat. These include the Egyptian mau, the Abyssinian, and the Burmese.

Egyptian mau

Burmese

Abyssinian

A New Mix

Cat lover Jean Mill founded the Bengal **hybrid**. In the early 1960s, Mill bought a female Asian leopard cat. The wildcat mated with a black **tomcat** and had a female kitten. The kitten grew up and had kittens of her own. Shortly after, Mill had to give up **breeding** cats.

Years later, Mill began working with Dr. Willard Centerwall. Centerwall wanted to address the problem of **leukemia** in cats. He knew Asian leopard cats did not get the disease as often as house cats. So, he crossed several Asian leopard cats with **domestic** cats.

Mill adopted Centerwall's hybrid cats. She wanted to use them to breed domestic cats that looked like wildcats.

In 1980, Mill found a domestic tomcat in India with a leopardlike coat. She took the cat back to the United States. There, she began breeding him with female

hybrids. Most modern Bengal cats can be traced back to that **tomcat** from India.

Experts said a wildcat and a house cat could not produce kittens. Yet they were wrong! Mill named her first hybrid Kin Kin.

BENGAL CATS

Mill was pleased the cats created from the **hybrids** made handsome pets. Today, many Bengal cat owners have realized the same thing. The Bengal cat looks like its beautiful, wild ancestor. However, it has the sweet temperament of a **domestic** cat.

The most striking feature of a Bengal cat is its coat. The coat is satiny and almost seems to shimmer. It is wild looking with either leopard spots or marbling.

The Bengal cat is a medium to large house cat. Its hindquarters are slightly higher than its shoulders. This hybrid has a thick tail, which it carries low. The Bengal cat also sounds slightly different from an ordinary house cat. It can coo and chirp!

Bengal cats are intelligent, lively pets.

BEHAVIOR

The behavior of the Bengal cat reflects its wild background. This **domestic** cat is quick and active. It likes to jump, somersault, and climb. The Bengal cat also loves water. In fact, this **hybrid** has been known to jump into a running shower!

In addition to its great personality, the Bengal cat is highly intelligent. It can be trained to walk on a leash. And, it can learn simple tricks such as rolling over.

Many families enjoy the Bengal cat's affectionate, playful nature. However, this hybrid is not a good fit for everyone. People who do not have time for play should not take on a Bengal cat. A Bengal cat will stretch out for a nap from time to time. But it prefers to be active.

The Bengal cat likes being with kids and grown-ups.

COATS & COLORS

The Bengal cat has been **bred** to look like a wildcat. Its thick, short fur is either spotted or marbled. Spots with at least two colors or shades in them are called rosettes. This pattern is especially popular.

The Bengal cat's coat tends to darken with age. Spots also become darker and more defined as the cat gets older.

Silver spotted Bengal

A popular color for the Bengal cat is brown **tabby**. This cat displays a yellow to orange coat with contrasting dark markings.

Mink marbled Bengal

Three other main colors are seal lynx point tabby, seal sepia tabby, and seal mink tabby. There are also snow leopard, silver, blue, and solid black Bengal cats.

The seal lynx point tabby displays an ivory to cream coat. This cat has tabby markings on the face, ears, paws, and tail. The seal sepia tabby and seal mink tabby coats are ivory, cream, or light tan. All three main colors have patterns in a variety of shades of brown.

17

SIZES

The Bengal cat is slightly larger than its Asian leopard cat ancestor. The Bengal cat's size comes from its **domestic** house cat background. However, a Bengal cat may appear larger than an ordinary house cat. This is because it has a long, muscular body like a wildcat.

Adult Bengal cats can range in size from 6 to 15 pounds (3 to 7 kg). Male Bengal cats usually weigh between 9 and 12 pounds (4 and 5 kg). Female Bengal cats normally weigh 7 to 10 pounds (3 to 5 kg).

Male Bengal cats stand about 9 to 11 inches (23 to 28 cm) tall at the shoulders. Their average length is 12 to 14 inches (30 to 36 cm).

**Smaller female cats are pregnant for about two months.
Larger wildcats are pregnant for about four months. At birth,
kittens are tiny and helpless. Their senses begin working
about 10 to 12 days after they are born.**

CARE

The Bengal cat loves attention. Owners must be prepared to spend time and energy playing with this active cat. They must also provide their Bengal cat with plenty of space and toys.

Like all house cats, the Bengal cat needs regular visits to a veterinarian. A veterinarian can provide these special pets with **vaccines**. He or she can also **spay** or **neuter** Bengal kittens at the proper age.

Daily needs for the Bengal cat include fresh water and high-quality food. Owners should also regularly brush their Bengal cat. And, they should give it an occasional bath. With proper care, a Bengal cat can be a loving family pet for many years.

Many Bengal cats love to curl up next to their family members at night.

20

GLOSSARY

breed - a group of animals sharing the same ancestors and appearance. A breeder is a person who raises animals. Raising animals is often called breeding them.

brush - low bushes or other vegetation.

domestic - tame, especially relating to animals.

Felidae (FEHL-uh-dee) - the scientific Latin name for the cat family. Members of this family are called felids. They include domestic cats, lions, tigers, leopards, jaguars, cougars, wildcats, lynx, and cheetahs.

habitat - a place where a living thing is naturally found.

hybrid - an offspring of two animals or plants of different races, breeds, varieties, species, or genera.

leukemia (loo-KEE-mee-uh) - a disease marked by an abnormal increase in white blood cells. Leukemia is a kind of cancer.

neuter (NOO-tuhr) - to remove a male animal's reproductive organs.

nocturnal - active at night.

plain - a flat or rolling stretch of land without trees.

rodent - any of several related animals that have large front teeth for gnawing. Common rodents include mice, squirrels, and beavers.

spay - to remove a female animal's reproductive organs.

tabby - a coat pattern featuring stripes or splotches of a dark color on a lighter background. Individual hairs are banded with light and dark colors.

tomcat - a tame male cat.

vaccine (vak-SEEN) - a shot given to animals or humans to prevent them from getting an illness or a disease.

WEB SITES

To learn more about Bengal cats, visit ABDO Publishing Company online. Web sites about Bengal cats are featured on our Book Links page. These links are routinely monitored and updated to provide the most current information available.

www.abdopublishing.com

INDEX